D1466331

FUNNY CARS

BY CAMERON STEELE

BELLWETHER MEDIA • MINNEAPOLIS, MN

Are you ready to take it to the extreme?
Torque books thrust you into the action-packed world
of sports, vehicles, and adventure. These books may
include dirt, smoke, fire, and dangerous stunts.
WARNING: read at your own risk.

This edition first published in 2011 by Bellwether Media, Inc.

No part of this publication may be reproduced in whole or in part without written permission of the publisher.
For information regarding permission, write to Bellwether Media, Inc., Attention: Permissions Department,
5357 Penn Avenue South, Minneapolis, MN 55419.

Library of Congress Cataloging-in-Publication Data

Steele, Cameron.
  Funny cars / by Cameron Steele.
    p. cm. -- (Torque: The world's fastest)
  Includes bibliographical references and index.
  Summary: "Amazing photography accompanies engaging information about funny cars. The combination of
high-interest subject matter and light text is intended for students in grades 3 through 7"--
  ISBN 978-1-60014-587-2 (hardcover : alk. paper)
  1. Funny cars--Juvenile literature. I. Title.
  TL236.23.V665 2010
  796.72--dc22
                                    2010034745

Printed in the United States of America, North Mankato, MN.

010111   1176

CONTENTS

What Are Funny Cars?

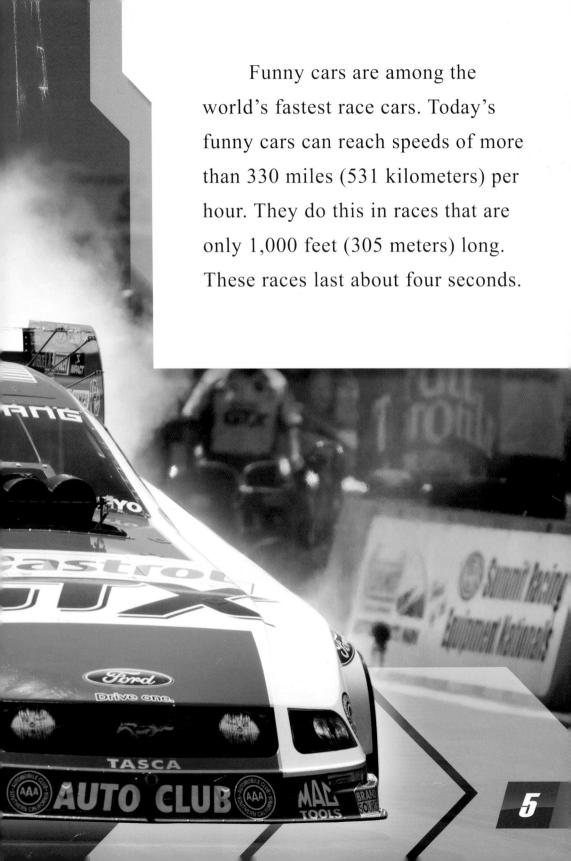

Funny cars are among the world's fastest race cars. Today's funny cars can reach speeds of more than 330 miles (531 kilometers) per hour. They do this in races that are only 1,000 feet (305 meters) long. These races last about four seconds.

A funny car gets its name from its strange look. Funny cars are long and low to the ground. They have large rear tires and brightly painted bodies. They look like stretched-out, muscular versions of normal cars.

Fast Fact

Funny car tires wear out after only four to six races, or about 2 miles (3.2 kilometers). Normal car tires can last up to 80,000 miles (128,748 kilometers)!

PRE-STAGE

STAGE

NHRA

Christmas tree

MOPAR

Fast Fact

Funny cars accelerate so quickly in such a short distance that they need parachutes to help them stop.

Funny cars compete in drag races. Two drivers race their cars on a **drag strip**. The cars slowly creep to the starting line. The drivers watch a tower of lights called a **Christmas tree**. Its yellow lights blink. Then the green lights flash! The cars roar down the strip. The first to reach the finish line is the winner.

Funny Car Technology

spoiler

Funny cars have cutting-edge technology that helps them reach their incredible speeds. Their bodies are made of **carbon fiber**. A funny car's body is 16 feet (5 meters) long, but it weighs less than 90 pounds (41 kilograms). A **spoiler** on the rear of the body creates **downforce**. This helps keep the car from lifting up off the track.

The body of a funny car can flip upward. This unique feature lets the driver climb into the **cockpit**. It also gives the **pit crew** access to the engine.

Fast Fact

A funny car has an escape hatch in the roof. The driver exits through the hatch in the case of an emergency.

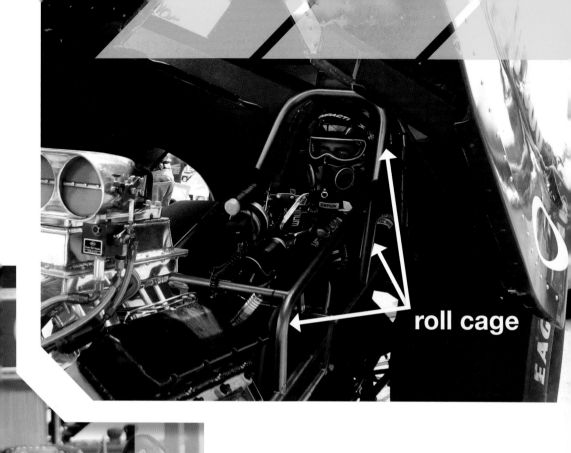

roll cage

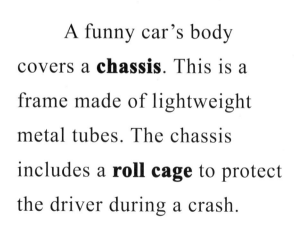

A funny car's body covers a **chassis**. This is a frame made of lightweight metal tubes. The chassis includes a **roll cage** to protect the driver during a crash.

A funny car's powerful engine sits in front of the driver. It is mounted to the chassis and includes a **supercharger**. This device mixes large amounts of air with **nitromethane** to create more **horsepower**. A funny car engine is over 40 times more powerful than a normal car engine!

Fast Fact

A funny car engine can cost as much as $50,000 and must be rebuilt after every race.

The Future of Funny Cars

Safety has always been a concern in funny car racing. The large engines and the use of explosive fuel increase the chance of accidents.

In 2008, officials decided to shorten many funny car races from the traditional 1,320-foot (402-meter) length. Shorter races mean less work for the engine. Officials hope shorter races will help prevent accidents.

Fast Fact

Drivers need to protect themselves in case of a fire. Funny car drivers wear helmets and fireproof suits, gloves, and shoes. The insides of funny car bodies are covered in a flame-resistant material.

John Force is a
drag racing legend.
He is a 14-time funny
car champion. In 2009,
his racing team and Ford Motor Company developed
the **Blue Box**. It collects information from the
chassis, engine, and tires. This information tells
race teams how to make future cars safer.

Fast Fact

Ashley Force Hood, John Force's daughter, holds the record speed of 316.38 miles (509.16 kilometers) per hour for funny cars at 1,000 feet (305 meters).

The National Hot Rod Association (NHRA) is the main organizer of funny car races. The NHRA works hard to keep drivers safe. In 2009, the NHRA made a rule that all funny cars must have a Blue Box.

The NHRA and people like John Force will make sure funny car fans enjoy the blazing speeds of these sleek machines for years to come.

GLOSSARY

Blue Box—a small box in a funny car that gathers information about the car's performance

carbon fiber—a strong material made by covering fabric with plastic

chassis—the frame on which a vehicle is built

Christmas tree—a tower of yellow, green, and red lights that helps start a drag race

cockpit—the area in a funny car where the driver sits

downforce—a physical force that pushes a car down to the track

drag strip—the straight, two-lane track on which funny cars race

horsepower—a unit used to measure the power of an engine

nitromethane—an explosive fuel that helps power funny cars

pit crew—the team members who help keep a funny car ready to race

roll cage—a cage around the cockpit that protects the driver during a crash

spoiler—a long, wing-like device that helps keep a funny car on the track

supercharger—a device that mixes large amounts of air with the engine's fuel to create more power

TO LEARN MORE

AT THE LIBRARY

Gigliotti, Jim. *Hottest Dragsters and Funny Cars*. Berkeley Heights, N.J.: Enslow Publishers, 2008.

Hart, Lou. *Drag Racing Funny Cars: Factory Flyers to Flip-Top Fuelers*. Hudson, Wisc.: Iconografix, Inc., 2008.

Von Finn, Denny. *Funny Cars*. Minneapolis, Minn.: Bellwether Media, 2010.

ON THE WEB

Learning more about funny cars is as easy as 1, 2, 3.

1. Go to www.factsurfer.com.

2. Enter "funny cars" into the search box.

3. Click the "Surf" button and you will see a list of related Web sites.

With factsurfer.com, finding more information is just a click away.

INDEX